https://www.facebook.com/smallfishbigpondpoetry/

Cover art: rudall30, istockphoto.com

FIRST EDITION

ISBN-13: 978-0-578-51713-1
ISBN-10: 0-578-51713-2

Bedroom Poems

By
SHANNON PHILLIPS

Small fisH
Big ponD

POEMS

"It was you who engineered
his mouth.

Tell me, Desire,
did you carve it out of his flesh
with your own forked sandpaper tongue?"

— Nadia Davi, *Desire of the Endless*

Endless Coupling

"Words are so erotic, they never tire of their coupling."
— Stanley Kunitz

It doesn't need to be in a bed. There's always the table,
a way to dine. Forget the fork—use only knife and tooth.

There will be plenty to drink, my tongue to lap at your lap,
yours to suggest I use my palm as spoon.

It doesn't need to be in a bed. It can be in front of the mirror—
set aside the comb, the perfume. Your face, my face—I *know* you.

I can tell you where to grab—where to strike and make it rich.
Make me rain while you reign, stake your claim on the moon.

It doesn't have to be in a bed. The floor is just fine.
My knees will forgive me. And if they don't—

the pain will remind me, scrawling from my spine,
its message in my skin will read *breathe* and soothe.

It doesn't need to be in a bed. The dishes need doing
and so do I. Bent, melded—we'll find a way to make do.

In the bed, before work, in the shower,
in the backseat, front seat too,

in the night, after dinner, put away the groceries,
forget about the TV, worship the morning dew:

we'll compose our couplets, endlessly
endlessly—combinations on loop, never not new.

Then and Now

You used to get so drunk off my skin you'd
hiccup between moans and every time you
closed your eyes, shadows were thrown
on the backs of your lids as if goddesses
were performing rituals inside your skull.

But now, I permeate you, a slow
warmth pooling at the bottom of your belly as
would an aperitif: cognac or perhaps brandy.
From there, I travel your limbs.
You sip me for an hour.

Dearly Beloved

He feeds her raspberries
dipped in cream.
His tongue, precise
as a diamond, traces
triangles until he
deciphers the code
that allows him to enter her
purple mood.

Her permission, more
precious than pearls,
than doves' tears, reflects
in her eyes, and wearing
a strand of dreams, her mind
fills with warm rain and sky.

Fucking

My feet bracket your ears,
my legs two trophies you palm,

your palms now fists, blunt
stakes in the mattress.

I could soak you up all day,
but you clicked us on,
plugged me in, unplugged the minute.

I'd talk dirty, but words flail,
only your name—
frayed, split, atomic.

Cobblestone

We eat hot crêpes at a wrought-iron café table outside
despite the cold,

our conversation no doubt noteworthy,
but can't compete

with hazelnut cream, the flush kindling your skin,
or with the impulse

to test the buoyancy
of your lower lip with my thumb.

I don't ask

the champagne
why it graces the glass
with its gold; or the glass
why it curves just so—

I don't ask why we stare
into the fire.

No, I don't ask the light
why it traces your face;

Nor do I ask about the warm
seam of our bodies,

why
we
fit.

Muse

What strange verse
did her perfumed
presence
stitch into your skin,
that sly calligrapher,
all scattered pulses
and breath.

One synaptic lick
from the hot goblet
of her mouth will
bring all your beats
back, fruit for fingers,
jeweled alphabet.

Untangle her
electric language
and she will sing
the ritual of your
vertebrae.

The Whole World

I can't write about war,
but I can write about your teeth
near my throat.

I can't write about religion,
but I can write about your voice
across the table at dinner.

I can't write about discrimination,
but I can write about your skin
pressed against mine.

I can't write about the economy,
but I can write about your hands
gripping my hips.

I can't write about technology,
but I can write about your spine
and the parallel canals I knead on either side.

I can't write about famine or drought,
but I can write about the sweat
at the small of your back.

I can't write about natural disasters,
but I can write about your mouth
taking me under.

Failing at English

I want to describe her legs as lusty,
as in: inspires my lust, but I can't.

Lusty is a state, not to be projected
on legs or hair or a look.

It also means robust:
She has robust legs that are lust-worthy.

"I feel lustful" does not work for me, either.

The same is not true for sexy.

Her legs can be sexy, I can be sexy,
I can feel sexy and I can be inspired
to think of sex

by looking at her legs.

Lingerie According to de Saussure

Black panties are not sexy.
They're not even black.
Or panties.
They are.
They.
The.
Th.
T.

Little French Maid of His Mind

with her black lace
and
clean lines.

No flaunt and fluff
today for her
white ruffles;

Today her time
belongs
to his piano—
all 88 keys.

She dips her tongue
into his
Cognac,
dip and lick

dip and lick

88 dips
88 licks

lick   dip
lick   dip

88 times

and he watches

even though
she always performs
her duty with
perfectionist

indulgence,

nuzzles
each of his notes
until she, not he,
is satisfied.

Afterward,
he takes her
cheek, taps
her temple and

instructs,
gently,

"Leave this dirty."

Whips & Chains

I.

He told me to scrub the pan.
I had offered really.

He said to make it impeccable.

Our versions of impeccable
weren't the same, but I scrubbed it anyway.
Twice.

I put it on the rack to dry.

II.

He called me into the kitchen.

Showed me how to use the point
of a steak knife to scrape off the grease
that had collected near the handle.

The pan clattered as he let it go in the sink.

Up against my backside, he belted his arm
around my waist, a chunk of me in his fist.

He accused me of doing it on purpose,
but I didn't mind
because his mouth was near my neck.

III.

I picked up the steak knife,
and wondered

if he really cleans his pans
so meticulously,

or if he's the one looking for an excuse,
to put his mouth near my neck.

Cannibal Romance

We had dinner once.

I ate off the plate of your back,
chewed your nipples like mushrooms,
sautéed in sweat sauce.

I even ate your scars,
peeled off each like thin licks of garlic.

The one from your first rugby injury
left a particular zing on my tongue.

I took a warm earlobe in my mouth
when it occurred to me that your spine
would make a fine dish rack.

Fantasizing at the Coffee Shop

Her attention was whisked away from a row of packaged coffee beans by a woman in line, and the long dark braid that hung like a sedated snake down the center of her back. She wondered if the woman enjoyed getting her hair pulled—bound for a firm yank right at the base. The braid was so long, a prospective puller might even grasp it first, then tightly coil it around a forearm for a more controlled rein. The right person would probably threaten to hack it off and use the severed braid as a whip. The right person *would*.

Lunch at the Mall Food Court

I know I'm supposed to look
at the woman in the architectural
pumps and pencil skirt, smooth
blouse and Pilates arms, the one
in line at Starbucks;

But I'm looking at the mom,
baby stroller on a casual course
in front of her, jeans a waterskin
of curves, fistfuls and then some,
to last even the greediest, grabbiest

luckiest bastard.

Just a Little Paunch

I used to date this guy.
He would take forty-mile bike rides
and eat soy snacks.

Whenever he hugged me,
he'd crack my back, and
tell me I needed to lose five pounds.

To which I'd always respond,
Women should be soft and curvy,
it makes them more fun in bed.

I wish I could've seen his face
the first time we had sex;
It was one of those things where he had

rolled over and spooned me
first thing in the morning,
wedging his cock between my thighs.

Automatically, he'd reached over
and molded his hand against my belly.
I thought I could sense his

split-second disapproval,
immediately followed by
a firmer, more assured press.

Coworkers

The afternoon sunlight glamorizes our
matching glass dishes,
but my chilled jewelry box of grapes glows
richer than his cherry tomatoes.

We eat where and when we can.

I ask if his wife packs his lunch.
He says she makes him eat what she calls
"clean" foods.

He slides the tomatoes over when he's had
enough;
our offerings clink like we'd toasted with
champagne.

"Don't mix them," he says. "You'll expect one
and get the other."

"My horoscope says I'm adventurous," I tell
him, opening my mouth to the possibility.

Plum

I stood in the break room with him while
he rambled on about flight reservations and
accrued vacation hours.

It was like waiting for water to still,
for the image to stop rippling,
for when I could finally focus.

The membrane of his lip was so delicate
I almost expected to catch a tiny flutter of a pulse
like at the dip in the bone where his throat
merged with his pectoral plate.

His lower lip in particular
such a ripened grape,
that if I barely made a tiny slice
with perhaps, say,
an Exacto knife:

It would burst.

A couple of coworkers everyone speculated were sleeping together
returned from a smoke break.

"Hey, do you want this plum?"
He was cleaning out his lunch box;
I'm sure he'd hate to throw away something
that was still good.

I plucked it from him,
wrapped it in a paper towel to keep it from getting marred,
and stashed it in my purse.

What anyone needed a mouth like that for, I don't know.

Office Space

The man I want would be able to resist
that alluring coworker.

Maybe she would have the same hair color
as the girl he had a crush on in high school,
all grown up in a pencil skirt, nude
nylons, a muscular carve up her calves
from wearing heels.

Before her manicured hands could slip
into his hair, drawing him to her,
he'd stop.

He'd be aroused,
might even admit to his temptation,
certainly to his being flattered—

I refuse to throw myself on men in copy rooms
to find him.

Subordinate

Every time I use a watercooler,
I think of him.

I didn't know how to use the hot
water nozzle.

He showed me,
mock consoling me.

"I'm sure you have other skills,"
he said.

After that, he would find out
what those skills were.

And no one would find out.

To the filet mignon left on my plate

I was spoiled, stuck up.
I was embarrassed because I talked too much.
Wine glasses mocked me at the table.

His hand smoothed the linen next to his wine glass.
Later, my ass would be stuck up, shaped by his hands.
I wanted to be cool and smooth in front of him, but my face

was difficult to control. I couldn't look at his eyes.
The light in the wine was in my eyes.
He knew he could fold me, knew that I would bend.

I wanted to be cool and smooth in front of him,
not like that steak on my plate, all that pink shame
out for everyone to see. I couldn't eat it.

Dirty Talk

I don't know why
the glaze that comes
over your eyes
makes me feel powerful,
but it does.

It's really just
your pupil growing
blacker.

Cocks are supposed to be
dumb, in their urge
toward wet heat,

but not faces.

Faces are supposed to be
articulate, reflecting
what goes on
behind your eyes.

But it's your cock
that shows me what's
really going on,

taking over
the role of your face.

Your eyes show *me*:

turning myself on,
turning your cock on,
and turning off

your face.

Bee-Stung Lips

What is so beautiful
about a bee sting
or a pout

is it
meat for teeth

Cupid cuts
teeth tease

the angle her body makes
he likes to see it

the color lux in her eyes
he wants to drink it

What is so beautiful
about a woman who wants

What is so beautiful
about a woman who hurts

Everyone knows a poem about sex is also a poem about death

after BH

Every hour begs to be inhabited,
known, not recorded. What if every
particle in an hourglass were a consonant,
a vowel in a poem written above
and unwritten down the center, made
and unmade, like love, like a bed,
like the shapes she makes
under his hands.

Remember that song and how it
curled around the moment,
a tongue unfurled, letting go
of words so to taste the sweetness
of what is fleeting.

Exquisite pleasure
is wedded to pain.

I met her at a BDSM club

I remember her hair was red

though I might have mixed this up
with the red leather of the St. Andrew's
cross she was strapped to.

Still, there was no confusing
the avalanche of cleavage that rushed
to the brim of her corset.

Thank God her eyes were closed, her body
enduring the exhale of a cat o' nine tails.

They say human ears can't handle
the sounds of heaven;
so much beauty is painful.

It isn't always about whips & chains

It wasn't her
lipstick-red nails on
milk-soft fingers,
busy in my harnessed
cleavage, protecting my
skin while unraveling
the evening's rope scheme.

It wasn't even that
she knew the difference
between good
and bad pain;

It was that she spent her
Saturday afternoons getting
hungry in used book stores
and that she made
the highest grade in her
Anatomy-Physiology
class at Cambridge,
receiving extra marks
for such keen
enthusiasm
in dissection.

Protégé

Five minutes is all it would take
to fall for his European-tinged mannerisms,
his professorial etiquette, gestures infused
with polite sophistication, the dark
hair adorning his forearms—

For once, I would like to show him
what I know.

I'd tie my legs around him, gentle as a ribbon,
all he'd feel is wet heat and maybe my hair
flick his collar bone.

For the penis I don't have

Penis Envy?
I don't think so.
Come on, it likes me better
than you anyway.

When it's in me, it's as good as mine;

Even when it's not in me all I have to do is
get on top and it sprouts from my pelvis
just as surely as from yours, squished ecstatically,
all that puppy enthusiasm.

The best part?

I don't have to deal with blue balls,
occasional mid-sleep eruptions,
inconvenient hard-ons; and a weakness
for just about any warm, wet place.

An Ode to Idris Elba's Torso

In the middle, beginning and end
of an expanse contoured for a pilgrimage,
a lion stretches in the sun.

Tonight

I could glide on your smile
slide right down
into an alternate universe

where
I lower myself onto your lap
where
I'm light as sweet smoke
where
the light in your eyes buoys me
where
my hands belong to your face
where

my kiss opens
                    and opens
again.

Tonight, I put my
desire
in your hands:

Make it dance.

ACKNOWLEDGMENTS

To Suzanne Allen, the ultimate muse; to Thomas R. Thomas for publishing my first chapbook, *My Favorite Mistake* (Arroyo Seco Press); to dancing girl press for publishing *Body Parts*, my second chapbook; to Patty Seyburn for prompting me to examine the violence in my poems (something I am still doing); and to Tony Barnstone for pulling me out of a buffet line and asking, "You're going to grad school, right?"

Also to George Hammons, Donna Hilbert, and Aruni Wijesinghe.

Some of the poems in this book first appeared in the following publications: *Cadence Collective, Chantarelle's Notebook, Crack the Spine, East Jasmine Review, Literary Review, The Rectangle, Tawdry Bawdry, Work to a Calm*, and with Washing Machine Press.

"Plum" took second place in Beyond Baroque's First Annual Poetry Contest.